MUSICAL INSTRUMENTS

© Rupa Classic India Series 1993
First Published 1993 by Rupa & Co.
7/16, Ansari Road, Daryaganj, New Delhi 110 002
Third impression 2000
Set in 9.6 on 12 Palatino by Printline, Daryaganj
Printed in India by Gopsons Papers Ltd., Noida
ISBN 81-7167-161-6

Photographs of musical instruments courtesy
SANGEET NATAK AKADEMI

Design: Pankaj Goel

MUSICAL
INSTRUMENTS

Photographs by Avinash Pasricha

Rupa & Co

INTRODUCTION

The musical instruments of India number at least 500. Their technical categorization is similar to that of musical instruments anywhere in the world, i.e., into chordophones, aerophones, membranophones and idiophones. However, Indian musical instruments in particular, must be seen in a wider perspective than a merely technical one. This is because Indian music itself carries a heavy freight of mysticism and esoteric description. For instance, within the context of Indian philosophy, religion and myth, the flute is not just a bamboo pipe that produces lilting notes. It is Krishna's call to Radha, the lover's call to the gopis (milkmaids) and the divine call to the human soul for union with God. Again, the veena is the instrument of the Goddess Saraswati and the sitar evolved from an ancient hundred-stringed lute created by the sage Narada to comfort the gods. Yet another legend, more secular in content, holds that the tabla was created by a pakhawaj player who, in a fit of temper, threw his instrument to the ground whereupon it broke into two pieces, thereafter referred to as the tabla and the bayan. The significance of these symbols and legends could be debated. What is verifiable is that several of these instruments date back to antiquity. This is apparent from the Natyasastra *(a treatise on the science of dramaturgy) which discusses the technique of applying paste on the tabla face and which was written as long ago as the 2nd century B.C.*

Shubha Mudgal

With its baffling technicalities, Indian music requires musicians to possess incredible skill. Mastery over the instrument is not the goal, however. In the Indian tradition, nada *(sound) is the very process of creation; the instrument is only the medium to a state of consciousness.*

The tanpura has a large gourd as a resonator. This is covered with a thin plate of wood. On the plate rests a bridge made of ivory, horn or wood over which pass four metal strings. A thread under the wires gives it its richness of sound.

Right: *M.S.Subbulakshmi*

Left: *Kishori Amonkar*

Overleaf: *Gangubai Hangal (vocal)*
Krishna Hangal (tanpura)

The tanpura is indispensable to most forms of Indian musical expression. It acts as an integrator, its drone providing the tonal backdrop.

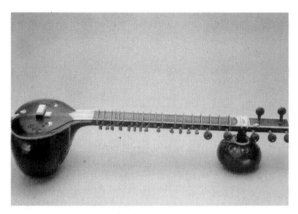

On the finger-board of the sitar are curved metal frets. There are five strings for the melody and two auxiliary strings used both for the drone and the accompaniment. Underneath the frets runs a set of thin wires tuned to the raga being played. These act as vibrators, enriching the sound of the instrument.

Right: *Vilayat Khan*

Below: *Nikhil Bannerjee*

Right: *Ravi Shankar*

The sitar is played with a wire plectrum (mizrab) worn on the forefinger of the right hand. Long, unbroken musical passages are rendered by stretching the string laterally against each fret. It is possible to produce upto six notes on a single fret.

The sarod has a small, deep body which is covered with parchment. Over the finger-board is a steel plate. A small metal bowl is screwed on at the end of the finger-board. The strings are plucked with a piece of wood. As in the sitar, there is a pair of drone strings and a set of thin wires.

Right: *Amjad Ali Khan*

The Saraswati or Carnatic veena has two gourds which give it increased volume. It is held across the body diagonally, with the upper gourd resting on the shoulder.

Below: *Doreswamy Iyengar*

Overleaf: *S.Balachander*

The finger-board of the veena has a number of frets which, in contrast to the sitar, are immovable. It has four strings and three auxiliary wires which form the drone.

The resonator of the sarangi is covered with skin. The strings are three in number with a set of thin wires under them. They are played with a heavy bow and by sliding the nails along the sides.

Overleaf: *Ram Narayan*

The jantra has twelve frets and two gourds. The two steel strings are at unequal height. The instrument is slung vertically around the neck and played with a curved bamboo bow.

Left: *T.N.Krishnan*

The violin has four strings. An import from Europe, it is not, however, tuned in the Western style; nor does the artist play it standing up but holds it between the right heel and chest.

Above: *N.Rajan and Sangeeta*

Right: *Lalgudi Jayaraman*

The violin is the only bowed instrument in Carnatic music for accompanying the voice as well as for solo playing.

The gottuvadyam is very similar to the Saraswati veena in construction but is without frets. Adjusting the pressure of the glass or wood slider along the strings is an extremely delicate process as the slightest change causes deviations.

Right: *Shiv Kumar Sharma*

The santoor has over sixty strings. It is played with two sticks that are curved at the ends.

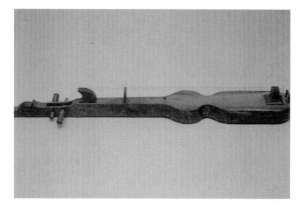

The nanduni has two steel strings tied on a peg box on
the upper side and to an iron hook bar at the lower end.

Right: *Pandit Jasraj*

The svaramandal, a small dulcimer, has about thirty
metal strings. It is strummed with the fingers.

Teejan Bai

The ek tara is one of the simplest of plucked instruments and is used only as a drone behind a melody. It has one string along a bamboo rod that is fixed to a gourd.

Overleaf: *The kamaicha is a lute-like instrument used by the Manganiyars, an itinerant group of musicians.*

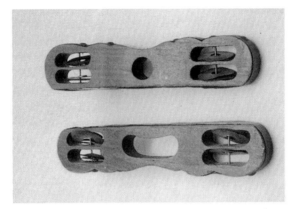

The kartals are used by the Manganiyars as well as the Langas, another group of musicians who move from village to village bringing song and music to the people.

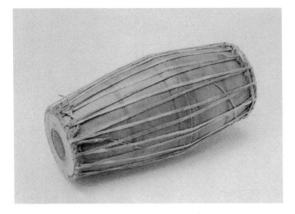

The mridangam is one of the oldest of Indian musical instruments and the most important percussion instrument in Carnatic music.

Overleaf: *L.Subramaniam (violin)*

Left to Right: *Tal Vadya Kacheri (mridangam)*

Vinayak Ram (ghatam)

The ghatam, a seemingly innocuous pot, can be a beautiful rhythmic accompaniment in the hands of an accomplished musician. It is made from a clay mixed with iron filings and is capable of an astounding variety of sounds and a very fast tempo.

Below: *Gayatri (Carnàtic veena)*

The two drum faces of the pakhawaj are held to the body by plaits and with each other by a leather strap. The cylindrical wooden blocks are used for tuning the instrument. Finer tuning is done by striking the plaits with a hammer.

Overleaf: *Ravi Shankar (sitar)*
            Alla Rakha (tabla)

Left to Right: *Trinath Maharana (pakhạwaj)*
Puranchand Majhi (harmonium)
Kailash Sharma (flute)
Saeed Zafar (sitar)

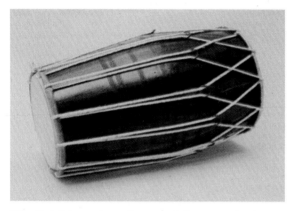

*The dholak is used mostly in the folk music of
North India. To achieve tonal variation between the two
heads, the left one is weighted with a paste. As a further
aid, the circular metal rings can be pulled to either side
to increase or decrease the tension.*

The pambai is composed of two cylindrical drums, each about a foot in length. It is hung in front of the body and tied to the waist. It is used as an accompaniment for folk dramas, ballads and religious rituals in South India.

The tasa is made of a clay bowl covered with parchment
and is played with a pair of curved sticks. The quality of
the skin, the diameter of the bowl and the method of
striking the parchment determines the quality of its
sound. It is used in processions and temple ceremonies
in North India.

The mandar is made of clay and has fine leather straps around its body. The right head is treated with iron filings and the left one with rice paste. Both are pitched to different tones. It is used in tribal dancing and group singing.

*The chenda is used in Yakshagana and Kathakali, both
dance-dramas of South India. Its rolling sound is so
powerful that it can be heard several miles off.*

The tabla is the most popular percussion instrument in Hindustani music. In a solo recital, the percussionist can exhibit his mastery over the instrument while in a concert he is required to possess the ability for alert adjustment with the main performer.

Right : *Zakir Hussain*

Overleaf: *Zakir Hussain (tabla)*

       V.G.Jog (violin)

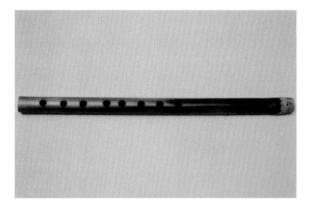

The bamboo flute is one of the most ancient instruments in the world. Played widely all over India, it is known by various names such as venu, vamsi, bansi, bansuri, murali in North India and pillankuzhal, pillanagrovi and kolalu in South India.

Below and overleaf: *Hari Prasad Chaurasia*

The large flute is perfectly suited to playing Indian classical music. Its flexibility of tone and range is similar to the human voice and exemplifies the vocal quality so prized in Indian music.

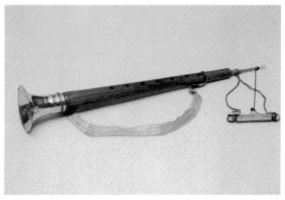

The shehnai is generally made of wood but may be of metal also. It has seven holes in it. At the blowing end are two flat pieces of reed with a small gap between them.

Bismillah Khan

The shehnai is associated with auspicious occasions such as weddings. Its intricate glissandos lend to it an emotive charm.

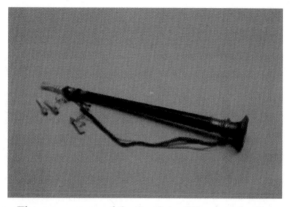

The nagaswaram of the South is of the same family as the shehnai of the North. The subtle graces of Carnatic music are brought out effectively on this instrument which, like the shehnai, is played on festive occasions. It is also used in temple music.